THE TIME IS NOW:

Developing Leaders for Today's Organizations of Color

DR. CASSANDRA Y. OWENS & HELEN J. OWENS

DR. NES INTERNATIONAL CONSULTING & PUBLISHING
LOS ANGELES COUNTY, CA

Dr. Nes International Consulting & Publishing
P.O. Box 70167
Pasadena, CA 91117
www.drnesintl.com

Legal Disclaimer: The sole purpose of this text is intended to inform and
empower the reader.

ISBN: 978-1-949461-12-1

Cover Photography: Stock Image
Cover Design: Michael Williams
Senior Editor: Kia Stokes

THE TIME IS NOW

Blank pages are intentional

DR. CASSANDRA Y. OWENS & HELEN J. OWENS

ACKNOWLEDGMENTS

As we prepared to write this book, we were able to speak with several persons in today's leadership sphere from various personal, professional, and organizational arenas. We are extremely grateful to those who offered and gave their assistance, advice, and insight. One of the most inspiring activity was reading and reflecting on the historical aspects of the leadership of organizations of color. It is our intent to fuse their perspectives with concepts and strategies of present-day leaders. We are grateful to them all.

Special thanks are given to:

Dr. Robert G. Owens, Sr., Our husband and father. He has been extremely patient during this project. Always the consummate professional, he provided advice and counsel as needed and allowed us to work long hours without complaining.

Womack and Edna Johnson , our parents and grandparents. They were sharecroppers during a large portion of their marriage. Neither one of them finished high school. However, both were incredibly gifted with wisdom and understanding and shared it willingly with all of us.

Elvira Nolan Owens , Cassandra's paternal grandmother. She was a strong-willed lady who lived far before her time. Her greatest gifts that she passed along were determination and integrity.

The next generation of the Robert and Helen Owens family who continue to make us proud.

Jordan C. Owens and Robert G. Owens III (Trey), Omaha, NE; LaNisha Owens, Mesa, AZ; Gabrielle Owens and Aryanna Owens, Lavergne, TN.

Dr. Clara D. Hewitt. She has always loaned her eyes, research skills, and wit to our projects and we are grateful.

Brenda Fuller, Fayetteville State University, Fayetteville, NC, a technology genius.

The late Bishop William H. Graves (retired), Mrs. Donna Bentley Graves, Jackie, Ameera, and William II. Bishop Graves was Dr. Owens' Best Man at his wedding and the family continues to be an integral part of our family.

Lane College, then and now, for all it has meant to our family.

Clark Atlanta University, for being a continuous model of teaching and executing exemplary leadership.

FOREWORD

Faith and Vision Congruent Factors in the Owens' Leadership Model

It has been my pleasure and responsibility to work with Helen Owens since we were in college together. We both held offices in student organizations. We collaborated within the faith community, and from the outside as professional colleagues. Her leadership in all instances clearly showed that she believed in fusing vision and faith as a major part of her leadership. This sets her apart as a leader, not only within the business and organizational world, but in the public-school systems in which she worked. This includes, but is not limited to, the higher education arena, local and state government, and church denominational service.

Upon assuming the leadership of Sigma Gamma Rho Sorority, Inc., a role that seemed to be designed for her, Owens immediately put into motion actions that would help the organization grow and expand its services around the world. Her tenure was marked by the capacity to seek consensus and she had the ability to compromise without losing face. But she also understood how to embrace the lonely and decisive moments when she had to stand alone and make the decision, she thought best for the organization. These crisis moments often did not allow a poll or vote to be taken.
It was at that time that she called upon her faith and sought God's perfect plan as she moved forward.

It has also been my great delight to watch her only daughter, Cassandra, follow in the leadership path her mother created. I often could not tell which one I was speaking with when I called their home. Cassandra has developed her own leadership style, but she, too, has distinguished herself as one of her generation's premier leaders.

While quick to affirm her faith, she depends on competence and preparedness as tools of her trade.

This describes, and maybe, defines Helen Owens and Cassandra Owens' leadership. As a member of a fraternity, I thank them for their vision and goals for the Sorority and the African American community. I am glad they had the ability to believe that God would allow them to see the manifestations of those dreams and visions. As a member of the Body of Christ, I thank them for their leadership blended with vision and faith; and for their desire to pass it on to the next generation of leaders. I thank them for dreaming big dreams and pray that the fruit of their labor will be long remembered.

William H. Graves[1]

Retired Bishop, Christian Methodist Episcopal Church

---

[1] Bishop Graves passed on November 30, 2019, before the release of this publication.

TABLE OF CONTENTS

CHAPTER 1

LEADERSHIP FOR YESTERDAY, TODAY, TOMORROW AND BEYOND

Often the question is raised, "What sets the most successful leaders apart from others?" Does it mean being an expert in the field? Or, the smartest person in the organization? While both are great accolades to earn, neither is a guarantee of leadership success. Simply put, leadership success means having high impact. *Ultimately, high impact leaders clearly define and orchestrate what happens next – in their organizations, their communities, and their world.*

We recall words from our father and grandfather, the late Womack Johnson, one of the informal leaders in the church and our community in rural West Tennessee. He said to us throughout his lifetime, "Dream with your eyes open."

This sounded contradictory to us as you are asleep most of the time when you dream. When we first heard this, we kept trying to explain to him why it made no sense to us. "Just keep on living", he would say to us when we would raise questions about the validity of this and some of the other statements he made. We know now he was saying to us what the writer of an old Negro spiritual meant when he wrote "We will understand it better by and by," and we do. Having been in leadership roles for many years, we understand that leaders of organizations, especially leaders within organizations of color, must keep their eyes open as they dream so they can see the opportunities and chances for advancement available to them and their organizations. But they must also be able to see the obstacles and roadblocks that may be in the way by accident or on purpose as they develop and pursue the organization's vision. These and many other admonishments were used and understood by the non-traditional leaders of the past and assisted them in determining the direction in which to go before the phrases of today were popularized. They must be remembered and serve as guideposts for today's leaders. It is incredibly essential for emerging leaders to learn from the history made by those who have gone before.

Difference between Leading Organizations of Color & Others

Leading organizations of color differs from leading organizations comprised of members who are primarily not of color. Organizations of color recognize that their communities are unique in their approach and needs. The organizations of interest in this book are historically African American based and led. However, in more cases than not, they are willing to partner with anyone, regardless of race, who believes in the organization's vision in order to enhance the probability of high impact.

One needs vision and an array of skills that are particularly well-suited for these times of changes and challenge. Thus, being adept to change is critical in a leader seeking to be uniquely excellent.

All too often, the leader prepares for the next meeting or event by looking at the agenda used last month or last year at this time, or for a similar event.

The activity is called to order and the assumption is made that everything must go according to the same dull script regardless of objective, previous outcomes, or current trends.

However, leadership and organizations today have lots of moving parts. Today's organizations may be viewed as microcosms, which for this purpose is defined as a small place, society, thing, or situation that has the same characteristics as something larger. In most cases, the parts reflect the whole. Some of the organizations operating today can be compared to small cities. The wise leader looks at all the parts and identifies the ones that have the most value to the success of the organization and allocates precious resources accordingly.

In their leadership model, *Healthy Relationship High Impact Leadership,* Owens and Owens have identified five significant and interconnected parts that are essential to most organizations of color:

1. *Healthy leaders*
2. *Healthy members*
3. *Healthy organization*
4. *Healthy partnerships*
5. *Healthy communities*

Figure 1: Owens & Owens' Healthy Relationship High Impact Leadership Model

Their research showed that once it has been determined that a real need exists in the community, defining the unique relationship(s) and strategic role(s) that each part plays in the success of the organization is a solid beginning point to high impact.

As shown in *Figure 1,* in order to have and serve a healthy community, a team comprised of healthy leaders who are well-prepared to perform the tasks associated with their office well, must be in place. However, for maximum effectiveness they must also be able to greatly influence the beliefs, behaviors, and practices of others. This is the foundation of organizational success.

High impact leaders make sound determinations regarding the other parts of the model.

Specifically, they are adept at determining those parts that present the most opportunities. They should also be able to make determinations regarding the parts that present the most challenges. Looking closely at the inside ensures that the organization is mostly comprised of healthy members who can exceed the standards set by the leadership team. This assessment allows for a healthy organization that has the capacity to run more smoothly, leverage an internal environment that generates productivity and good relationships (internally and externally), and is poised to make the impact it strives to attain in the communities served. Thus, the astute leaders should work on those concepts to create a healthy internal organization before moving to the external sphere.

Developing partnerships and expanding services into the community may be a means of increasing the viability of the organization as well as assisting in community growth in its efforts to reach identified goals. Therefore, the high impact leader will intentionally identify opportunities to form healthy relationships that may lead to partnerships in the community.

Before any commitment is made it is important to document and strengthen, if necessary, the services your organization can provide as a single entity, both in quantity and quality. This may require an informal assessment to ensure that you (or anyone on the leadership team) do not commit the organization to something that cannot be delivered. An unhealthy organizational commitment can be very detrimental to an organization.

High impact leaders have strong negotiating skills that enable them to build and maintain partnerships with other healthy organizations that can assist with the goals of your organization while building community.

When necessary, the leader should provide adequate education and training for the members of the team that may need additional competencies, particularly in areas that require members to be self-sufficient or to represent the interests of the organization. It is recommended that the leader actively participates in but does not dominate the training initiative/session in order to produce a healthier working environment and to gain insights and agreements on best practices.

This often gives the community increased awareness of the services offered by your organization and may lead to increased support.

We present this caveat. Establishing enduring contact with community-based organizations is often different and sometimes more difficult for leaders of organizations of color. This may not be the easiest entrance because the level of contact between members may be different or less meaningful. Therefore, leaders who wish to establish workable relationships must be intentional in developing healthy relationships with intended partners. As the leader, it is important to use every opportunity to get your name and the name of your organization in the public's eye in a positive manner. Join other organizations and volunteer for leadership roles so that others are aware of your skills and how you can help build a healthy community. During engagement, never let yourself be perceived as the weakest link in any setting.

Those who seek positions of leadership must continually work to make their organizations better and more capable of serving their present age effectively. This is particularly true for leaders of organizations of color.

The capability to provide service to ourselves, our members, the community, and beyond is elevated and the effects are more significant as we work to enhance our own capabilities. Leadership must be developed that allows for retaining membership and keeping the organization viable while often having to swim with external groups for funding and support.

So, it is then that as we make ourselves better, we continue to prepare for our today and tomorrow, but also for someone else's future.

It is of extreme importance to understand this truth:

There is no one right, most effective, or best way to lead. The journey to effective leadership has many paths that are available to the person seeking to be an extraordinary leader within an organization.

Those who seek positions of leadership must continually work to make their organizations better and more capable of serving their present age effectively. This is particularly true for leaders of organizations of color. The capability to provide service to ourselves, the community, and beyond is elevated and the effects are more significant as we work to enhance our own capabilities.

While some leadership roles are formal positions that require exerting authority, making decisions, taking responsibility, and delegating duties, others are less formal and may be assumed by a person who holds no formal position but has an inherent ability to influence organizational engagement, propose and direct strategies; listen and negotiate laterally, and synthesize a wide range of ideas into a cohesive plan. People who can do both exceptionally well are considered high impact leaders.

Two kinds of high impact leadership exist: *visionary leadership* and *direction-finding leadership*. Visionary leadership is based on a leader's passion and strengths whereas direction-finding leadership is based on the organization's members passion and strength. Let us discuss each in turn and how they are exemplified in organizations of color.

TWO TYPES OF HIGH IMPACT LEADERSHIP

Visionary Leadership

Many of yesterday's leaders are called visionary leaders. However, when considering the term "visionary leadership", defining it was difficult. Coming up with words that were appropriate to define it always seemed to leave a void. Then, the words of Duke Ellington, the late jazz musician, composer, and well-known band leader came to mind. He was asked to define the word rhythm. "If you got it," he said knowingly, "you don't need no definition. And if you do not have it, ain't no definition gonna help." The same is true for visionary leadership.

An attempt to define it is probably even more difficult than clearly defining the musical term rhythm.

Usually one will give a description of the word rather than a definition. The same will probably be done here.

However, it is safe to say that when we speak of visionary leaders, we think of people who can:

- set a vision that inspires others to act
- engage in productive interpersonal exchange
- create influence over any constituency or audience
- make powerful impressions on the people with whom they communicate
- forge productive relationships

Although the vision of what can and should be accomplished is set at the top, visionary leadership is demonstrated throughout the organization. The vision that a leader has is often determined by what is viewed as the future common good for the organization. A quote from *Alice in Wonderland* gives another view of the importance of leaders having vision. Alice learned this lesson as she was seeking a way out of *Wonderland.* Upon coming to a fork in the road she knew she had to decide which way to go.

She said:

> *Would you tell me, please, which way I should go from here?" she inquired of the Cheshire Cat. "That depends a good deal on where you want to get to."* The Cheshire Cat answered. Alice told him that she did not really care too much. The smiling cat told her in a very definitive manner, *"Then it doesn't really matter which way you go."* Another wise writer said it this way, *"If you don't know where you are going, any road will take you there.*

Those in formal leadership positions must share and promote the vision in their daily decision making and in the evaluation of strategic opportunities. Their leadership success largely depends on their ability to ensure that the membership remains loyal to the vision and knows where it is going.

Direction-Finding Leadership

The value in direction-finding leadership is the embrace of change. Forward thinking, solution-oriented leaders do not stand still long.

The key to becoming a direction-finding leader is the ability to not only reflect the organization's principles and values, but also anticipate and adjust to a rapidly changing environment. Today's leaders must recognize that truly "Everything must change. Nothing stays the same."

These are the words to a song that was written by Bernard Ighner and recorded in 1978 by Nina Simone. It remains a favorite and has been sung by several artists. The direction-finding leaders must always keep this in mind. They must continually look for new routes to take the organization into these constantly changing environments.

There will be times when the question must be asked, "Which way should we go now?" The route will not always be clear, and sometimes there will be no road. Direction-finding leaders must be capable to proactively sense and frame the opportunities for the organization for today and for the future. They must be able to:

- see and plan for events and activities beyond the confines of today
- maximize natural talent of the organization's members, and work to expand capabilities
- develop solid decision-making ability
- recognize and develop other leaders

- navigate at every altitude
- live beyond oneself

Direction-finding leadership requires looking ahead instead of spending time on "what might have been," or "if only that had been done differently."

Furthermore, individual and group cultural habits are hard to break. Holding on to the past is natural and even comfortable for many people. An attachment is made to the people we were yesterday, and the things we used to do. But the leader who tries to re-create the organization or company's best times of the past will usually fail, because the world has moved on to a different place.

Likewise, the leader who allows past mistakes to set the parameters for today's achievements is making a big mistake. Direction-finding leaders let go of the past, good or bad, and work for a better future.

Regardless of which leadership model is deemed most beneficial, visionary or direction-finding, whether you are in a leadership position, or desire to hold one, remember the road to success always begins with a vision. George Washington Carver, brilliant scientist and educator, spoke to the importance of vision.

He said, "Where there is no vision, there is no hope." In order to keep the hope of your constituents in a good place, it is good to have a solid answer to this question, "What kind of organization do I want to lead?"

There is no better way to develop your vision and plan than to have a real answer to this question with specifics about each aspect of the organization. And do not forget to keep your eyes open as you dream. A sound vision is the key to unlocking innovation and creating a responsive organizational culture. They are paramount to developing an environment for optimal impact in this evolving technological, global, and diverse society.

This enormous responsibility will require urgency, relentless work, and intentional planning for finding meaning in all that is done. We can learn from history so that we do not repeat mistakes of the past.

HISTORICAL REVIEW OF ORGANIZATIONS OF COLOR

Historically, African American clubs and organizations had multiple purposes for their existence. The tapestry making up the history of the organizations of color has been woven from many pieces of fabric and many threads.

Likewise, the visionary leadership that led to the establishing of churches, clubs, fraternal Greek-lettered-organizations, fraternal orders of masons, political groups, and others for people of color goes back to many reasons, circumstances, and locations. Much of the leadership came about because of necessity. There was a grave need for leadership, and a person emerged from the ranks.

The meetings, most of the time, became multi-faceted business and social settings with mostly invited African Americans in attendance. Time, occupations, and limited resources did not allow for a lot of different activities within the community. Therefore, these meetings became the hub of the social set as well.

This socio-corporate characteristic often carries over into today's organizational culture. So, it must be viewed from several perspectives. It is sometimes a hindrance, but many leaders have made it work for them. The social piece can become a growth mechanism for the organization by blending the more formal business culture and the historical social climate into a workable and productive fabric.

An examination of the writings of many African American historians can form the basis for a look at today's African American leadership.

A review of the February 1940 *Negro History Bulletin* written by Carter G. Woodson noted historian, author, and journalist, reveals that it is a most stimulating document.

It is apparent that Woodson placed great emphasis on the core values that are the foundation upon which today's leadership rests. These tenets are still far reaching and necessary for those who seek excellence in leadership. Woodson admonished his fellow Americans of color: "Do not let the role you have played be obscured while others write themselves into the background of your story."

It is from this backdrop that homage is paid to the men and women who pulled together loosely connected organizational structures whose genesis began from a need to help men and women of color affirm a degree of pride in their shared identity. Prevailing and sometimes strident conversations which centered on issues such as race identity, establishing self-determination, religious freedom, and gaining respect as a people were the impetus for the development of these newly formed organizations.

The leaders of current organizations of color stand on the shoulders of many individuals and groups who had the courage to pull together to ensure the imprint of their history was recorded and acknowledged.

Building on the Past

How can one build on what has been done to make the organization and the community it serves a better place? How can help be given to assist members in feeling more ownership of what was initially envisioned? What is the level of leadership that leads to real progress in today's world? How does one serve the present age in this new millennium? What will it take and how can today's leaders make tomorrow better?

It is recognized that today's questions can often be answered by looking at yesterday's solutions. It is clear in studying and assessing leaders of the early established organizations that they did not embrace nor accept mediocrity in their achievements. The steps they took to establish the organizations indicate they were people who understood excellence, in their own way, in every definition of the word.

Because they understood how to lead in never before navigated waters, they laid a foundation for solid leadership that has remained for nearly a century. Many of their strategies are powerful for today's leaders of organizations of color as they confront issues from within and from outside of the organization.

A review of the past makes it clear that leaders of color were called at that time in history to lead and serve in difficult circumstances. In the same way leaders of color have an important role to play in the 21st Century. However, today's leaders must be enabled and equipped with the competencies necessary to perform skillfully in a global society. It is necessary for the leaders to be change agents who impact the organizations, their communities, and the world.

Perhaps one of the most celebrated visionary leaders within organizations of color was Reverend Dr. Martin Luther King, Jr., noted preacher and civil rights advocate. Dr. King said it this way when speaking of the individual commitment, "An individual has not started living until he can rise above the narrow confines of his individualistic concerns to the broader concerns of all humanity."

While these words appear to be those of a direction-finding leader, Dr. King is considered visionary because his vision for America, if not the world, was considered such a drastic change that even people within his own community questioned his efforts.

On the other hand, General Colin Powell, an iconic military leader and exemplary path-finding leader, handed down thirteen rules in his book, *It Worked for Me in Life and Leadership*. Powell also says that leaders should remember that "Your past is not necessarily your future." Powell's lessons, tried and true, provided some insights for leaders at all levels seeking to make high impacts regardless of organizational settings.

Businesswoman, actress, and philanthropist, Oprah Winfrey is a juxtaposition of visionary and path-finding leadership. Oprah, living proof that King's vision for African Americans can be realized, asserts that "It doesn't matter who you are, where you come from. The ability to triumph begins with you. Always." Leaders who wish to move to the next level are intentional about expanding their capacity to perform in leadership roles within their organizations.

Some leadership roles are classified as those that facilitate execution of the organization through building alignments, winning mindshare, and growing the capacity of others. Developing appropriate high impact leadership behavior for the situation is a continuing journey, but it will be good for the person and the organization.

Everyone will not reach the same level of effectiveness, but everyone wishing to lead should seek to develop essential leadership skills.

CHAPTER 2

INVESTMENTS IN YOURSELF

In preparation for this book project, we discovered a plethora of sources related to leadership. Various genres provided everything from descriptors of principles of leadership, leadership styles, to management techniques, all in hopes of molding a better leader. Every leader or aspiring leader should continually learn from yesterday's great leaders to develop and grow their leadership skills. Each leader has a place or role in his or her organization or community, and each is as different as the group that is led. A well-remembered homily that our mother and grandmother, the late Edna Johnson, recited to us is, "The cream will rise to the top."

Our experiences taught us that after the cream got to the top it thickened and became richer so that is could maximize its assignments.

Excellent leadership is much the same. Getting to the top, then and now, is only getting to first base. Invest in yourself to ensure that you stay abreast of best practices, current trends, and changing environments that may affect you or your organization positively or negatively.

There is, however, one principle of leadership that must be understood. That is, all leaders must develop and grow their own leadership style. Every leader needs to have a style that is unique and takes into consideration all individual personal strengths and weaknesses. But leaders should not use individuality as an excuse for incompetence and inadequacy. Often the phrase, "That's just the way I am", is used as a justification for inappropriate or mediocre leadership. However, excellence in themselves and the organization should be the standard for each leader.

Defining Your Personal Organizational Vision

When thinking about the terms describing organizations and organizational leadership two questions usually come to mind. The first is, "What kind of organization is it?" And the second one is, "Who is the leader?"

Inherent in these questions is, "What is this organization about and where is it going under the leadership of its chosen leader?"

Answering the first question is somewhat easy. You can examine mission statements and archival data to learn a great deal about what an organization values and its accomplishments. Empowered with this information you can develop an organizational vision. Organizational vision is a mental image of a possible and desirable future for the organization.

The leader may picture growth in:

- membership numbers
- finances
- services
- program development
- real estate holdings
- other aspects of the organization

The leader who is going to make a visible difference must be able to set the vision, chart the course and move the people forward. While this may require free style leadership, the leader must have clarity regarding the direction the organization will go. However, before these key drivers of success can be communicated to others, the leader needs a clear vision about the plan for leading the organization in general.

This will ensure that the leader will be better equipped to inform followers and members about how their organization's vision can be achieved.

However, many leaders tend to focus on an organization's mission and vision prior to developing an organizational vision that defines them as leaders irrespective of the organization in which they lead.

This is a mistake. When an organization selects someone as their leader, they should have a clear understanding of the leadership values and how issues are addressed in the leadership role. This is the vision that the leader will promote during any interviews, campaigns, and meetings if selected to lead.

Developing Appropriate Leadership Skills

It is easier to succeed when one's strengths and weaknesses are identified. This allows the leader to maximize the use of the strengths, talents, and gifts for the good of the organization. Similarly, one will encounter fewer problems if areas of weakness are known. This will ensure that the leader manages the weaknesses rather than the weaknesses doing the managing.

A personal *Strengths, Weaknesses, Opportunities, and Threats* (**SWOT**) analysis can be a useful technique that helps identify where one is in each of these categories.

This assessment allows the leader to further develop the individual talents and abilities needed to advance the organization and help one achieve personal goals. The SWOT assessment can also help identify, manage, and eliminate threats that might otherwise hurt your ability to move forward personally and ensure that the organization stays on the right course. The areas of strength can become the framework for the continuing development of leadership skills.

Some questions that may be asked in each area:

STRENGTHS

- What do you do well?
- What advantages do you have that others do not have, i.e., skills, education, certification, connections?
- Of which of your achievements are you most proud?
- What values do you hold that most others do not exhibit?
- Do people like you at first sight?

WEAKNESSES

- What tasks do you avoid because you do not feel confident doing them?
- What are your negative work habits (for example, are you often late, are you disorganized, do you get angry quickly, are there problems with handling stress)?
- Are there personality traits that hold you back in your field or position,(i.e., excessive shyness, fear of public speaking, overly aggressive, self-centered)?
- Do other people speak of weaknesses that you do not see?

OPPORTUNITIES

- Do you know some strategic contacts that may be helpful to you?
- Can your technological literacy help you?
- Is your organization growing? How can you use this to your advantage?
- Do you have useful skills that others do not have?

THREATS

- What obstacles do you or the organization currently face?
- Does changing technology threaten your position?
- Is the demand for your skills changing?
- Could any of your weaknesses lead to threats?

Utilizing a SWOT analysis will often give key information that can help in leadership development. It can point out what needs to be done in each area and put problems into perspective. It can also inform you of competitive advantages and disadvantages that can be leveraged or will need immediate attention.

It is important to identify strengths and develop them to the fullest. The recognition of weaknesses is important because then ways can be found to build them up as much as possible. This is the path to high performance. Excellent leadership skills are necessary for ensuring that one's performance is always of high quality, and to enhance the organization's growth and vitality.

In additional to conducting a personal SWOT analysis, consider the following assessment which not only evaluates the leader but requires you to examine the organization and its members as well.

A Reflective Look at You, Your Organization, and Your Members About You

1. What are three strong points about your leadership?
2. What are three things that you can control that you will work on to make you a better leader?

3. What are three things that are out of your control that could make you a more empowered leader?
4. Who was a strong influence in your leadership development and why?
5. Comments (include other comments that were not already addressed)

About Your Organization

1. In what areas/foci does your organization work?
2. What are three strengths of your organization compared to other organizations within the same areas/foci?
3. What can you do to cause the organization to improve?
4. How do you want your organization to grow?
5. Why do you want your organization to grow?
6. Comments

About Your Members

1. What are five to seven descriptors that define your members' identity?
2. How do you build strong relationships among your members?
3. List three principles that will make better members.
4. What is most valuable about your members?
5. Comments

The question is often asked about a list of good leadership skills one should have in order to be an excellent leader. That is a difficult one because the use of leadership skills can be dependent on the situation and the individual handling the situation.

So, it is important to establish up front that there is no *one* set of leadership skills that will guarantee success. However, any leader or aspiring leader should develop a leadership skill set that will enable successful interactions with supervisors, employees, colleagues, clients, and others in the organization and beyond.

Spoiler Alert! Please do not expect to excel in all the leadership qualities, characteristics, and traits seen in this area. This will be an impossible task, and it may become too stressful to be an effective leader. This causes some to give up on the task.

It is interesting to note that many who were considered great leaders were lacking in some of the skills and characteristics that are essential. But they recognized their strengths, worked on their weaknesses, and developed strong performance teams to help to meet the goals.

Leadership Checkers or Chess: Short-Term or Long-Term Goals

Leadership is much like the games of checkers and chess. Checkers and chess are both board games that require strategic moves and playing to conquer the opponent to win. Checkers winners usually facilitate a series of moves looking for the short-term advantage. Thus, the checkers game does not last long. Chess players are taught to play for the long term. Their strategy does not just look at the impact the move will have on the next play, but rather, how it will affect the board play and create advantage as the game proceeds.

Effective leaders seek to become chess leaders and develop strategies that are good for today but will also pay off down the road. This means seeing farther than just the next move. It also implies that the leader is planning for the organization's next moves after this one is facilitated.

This includes a determination of the moves that may be good for individual development, and for the organization and a real hard look must also be given at the potential moves that are available to the competition and how planned moves will impact them.

As with most endeavors and particularly with chess, learning the basic rules of the game is of primary importance. Just as there are basic rule books for chess beginners, there are basic guides for those who wish to become leaders, but feel they are insufficiently equipped to do so. The basic rules and conventions that govern chess play are expected to be known and adhered to by all players. So therefore, it serves to follow that new or less experienced players must spend some time in an intensive reading, learning and research mode. Those who desire to lead or who are new at the game of leadership must spend some time learning the basic rules of the game.

No one should allow themselves to be elected or appointed to an office without knowing or learning the basic requirements for that office. For example, it is an imposition on the membership or employees for one to be elected president or selected chairperson and does not know how to plan an agenda or carry a motion.

Just as with chess, aspiring leaders should take extra effort to ensure real knowledge and understand basic leadership rules and roles and how to best facilitate them.

However, there are times when the checkers strategy must dominate, and the planning must be focused on the short-term goals. It is important to have strategic plans ready for these times. Though, a series of short-term goals should not be the primary leadership plan.

Some people have maintained unfavorable opinions about chess and have developed a negative perception of the age-old board game and its players. Fortunately, for those who enjoy the game none of these sentiments are strong enough to tarnish or eradicate the game. Some of these myths run parallel to myths about leadership. Likewise, leaders should not be discouraged by myths about your leadership.

Myth #1: Chess is a difficult game/Leadership is a difficult process

Both chess and leadership often have an intellectual aura that implies they are activities in which only the best and the brightest can participate.

This is one of the main reasons why some individuals do not participate in either of them. The misconception is that both are overly complicated and not worth the effort is vast.

Both chess and leadership can be complex and can be deep. These are identified characteristics of the game and the process of leading. However, to be effective at either, one only must learn the basic rules. One must learn the basic chess rules to enter the game. With chess, knowing the basic rules will provide the foundation to improve and to ultimately face with a grandmaster. In the same manner, knowing the basic parliamentary rules constitute the fundamental knowledge needed to become a good novice leader. Most aspiring leaders can learn to provide solid leadership for any organization with a sound parliamentary background.

Myth #2   Chess is for smart people only/Leaders must be the smartest in the group

This may be the most prominent reason why some people do not even bother to try chess or leadership which is unfortunate for all.

In either the game or the leadership process one only needs enough brain cells to learn the basic rules. Usually it is certain that the capability of fending for oneself can be developed. Intellectual capability is important, but it is not enough to ensure success as a chess player or a leader. One must have a strong grasp on the rules and even the implications of the guidelines to be successful.

Myth #3:   Chess is just a game/Leadership is just a political game

This myth may be the most hurtful for the game and its avid players and followers as well as for leaders, aspiring leaders, and organizations. Chess is a game; that is true. What is not true is that it is only a game. With all the complexities within it and the depth of skill that one must put into chess it is more an art than anything else.

So, it is with leadership. However, leadership is much more than a political game. In chess, the rook has the lowest point value in the game. It is the foot soldier on the board and always the first to fall. As the leader of your group you will need to make sure your organization is not being positioned to be the rook, doing the initial hard work only to be pushed aside later.

There are political implications that must be studied to ensure that your organization is kept where it can move. And before you think about using another organization or individual for your own personal gain, consider if the consequences are worth it. You could lose the trust of other organizations or individuals and gain a less than desirable reputation through making bad political decisions. A good leader will develop the same art for interpretation and making good moves as the astute chess player in order to be successful. Moreover, a good leader can be displaced due to political moves that deliberately undermine their efforts in order to replace them with someone who is deemed malleable to the political whims of the organization.

The solid leader must also be aware of the different implications that are inherent in any decision made and the possible long term and short-term ramifications.

Good leadership requires viewing each situation from the standpoint of its impact within the organization as well as its external consequences.

So, to view leadership as just a political game is a mistake that many leaders make that keep them from rising to levels to which their abilities would take them.

These myths keep many people from trying the game of chess or seeking leadership roles. But there are those who find both to be some of their most fruitful endeavors. They take the time to learn the rules and develop into avid and good chess players.

In the same way, leaders are still being developed and stepping forward to take the helms of organizations. But there are still negative effects that come from wrong ideas concerning the role and requirements of leaders that cause many capable people to be put off and not play chess or seek leadership positions.

CHAPTER 3

SOME USEFUL LEADERSHIP SKILLS

While the leadership of the Board of Directors is assigned to the President, CEO, or Chairperson, the elected officers on the Board have the function of representing all members of the organization and managing the affairs of the organization. To be effective, officers must know the scope of their role and responsibilities. Therefore, aspiring leaders who wish to seek an office should learn as much about the requirements for that office as possible. In addition, they should become proficient in carrying out the duties of the office before becoming a candidate for that office. This investment in oneself will pay off as a creditable board member, more productivity for the organization, and skills that are transferrable to other places.

Productive and effective officers focus their attention on items of critical importance, rather than trivial matters. They are expected to understand the organization and their roles, to develop a strategic plan for their office that fits into the organization's mission and goals and be a part of the overall planning process.

The Leadership should develop a set of core values for themselves which may include:

- an active environment that is productive, growing, and welcoming
- consistent quality service to the members, partners, and each other
- engaging opportunities that promote member and organizational growth, develops leadership, and enhances the brand
- an atmosphere that provides an inclusive approach embedded in the actions, visions, and services that recognizes and honors the group's diversity.

In his quest to become the President of the United States of America, it is said that Barack Obama, the 44th President, changed the concept of leadership around the world.

In his book, *Leadership the Obama Way: Lessons on Teambuilding and Creating a Winning Culture in Challenging Times*, much attention is given to developing the appropriate skills for extraordinary leadership. He suggests that leaders hone their skills including how to:

1. Communicate your vision in clear, persuasive language
2. Create a "reservoir of goodwill"
3. Form and provide leadership for outstanding teams
4. Harness and leverage the power of technology
5. Establish trust and confidence
6. Build bridges among diverse people and organizations

In the 21st Century, organizations that had strict requirements for memberships are now faced with determining how to embrace people without focusing on differences that are not pertinent to their organizational success.

The ability to identify and build on strengths and transform weaknesses into strengths increases confidence and the proficiency to influence.

The complexities of today's global environment require leaders to continually acquire and hone new skills for high impact leadership.

Believe it or not, great leaders are not always born with the necessary skills to lead organizations well. Often, they create themselves by working on their personal and professional skills. A good leader and a Board of Directors that is willing to invest in themselves to be sure they have the needed skill set for their job will be a crown jewel for any organization.

Lisa Bing, noted educator, corporate consultant, and founder of *Bing Consultant Group, Inc.* talks about "Big Picture Leadership" in her five-part *Black Enterprise.Com Leadership Series.*[2] According to Bing, *Big Picture* or strategic thinkers see implications of their actions and decisions and come up with innovative solutions and new possibilities.

Thinking Big Picture– Lisa incorporates the classic story told by Stephen Covey about a diligent group of workers, who after an incredible amount of time of labor, discovered the group was working at the wrong location. Their discovery was invaluable. The insight they gain is something we all can learn from.

---

[2] See details here: https://www.blackenterprise.com/big-picture-mentality-how-to-develop-strategic-leadership-skills/

According to this series, Bing suggests, that leaders who want to be *Big Picture* thinkers should:

- Anticipate opportunities and potential problems (like the group of workers)
- Build productive relationships
- Reduce labor intensity
- Make sense of data
- Make connections among ideas and people that do not seem obvious
- Avoid or reduce conflict
- Stay ahead of the competition

In developing a "Big Picture" mindset, Bing suggests that leaders must be genuinely curious and interested in the group. Leaders must understand what each player is doing and what motivates them to be a part of the team. Though goals are important, they must be understood in relationship to the greater good of the entire team or organization.[3]

It is important for all leaders and potential leaders to know that all the leadership skills development available will not guarantee success. Nelson Mandela, former President of South Africa, said

---

[3] Ibid.

it this way: "Do not judge me by my successes. Judge me by how many times I fell down and got back up again." Be prepared to fall down many times in the leadership process but be equally prepared to get back up each time.

Great leaders understand and operate with this principle. Theodore Roosevelt, who at age 43 became the 26th and youngest President of the United States in its history, encouraged the 'Get Back Up Again Theory' in this manner:

> It is not the critic who counts, not the man who points out how the strong man stumbles, or where the doer of deeds could have done them better. The credit belongs to the man who is actually in the arena, whose face is marred by dust, and sweat, and blood; who strives valiantly, who errs, who comes short again and again, because there is no effort without error – who at the best knows in the end the triumph of high achievement, and who at the worst, If he fails, at least fails while daring greatly.

Rules of Engagement

As with all endeavors, learning the basic rules of the game should be of primary concern in leadership. This is particularly the case for those who intend to move up the ladder to top leadership positions.

Getting to know the rules and conventions of leadership should be the initial and most important step in preparing for leadership roles.

Any leader or aspiring leader and, particularly leaders of organizations of color, should learn the basic tenets of parliamentary procedures. This is necessary because the leader should know how to create orderly, effective, and productive meetings. In order to do this, it is helpful for those leading and those involved to know something about parliamentary procedures. In fact, history tells us that Henry Martyn Robert, soldier, engineer, and author, decided to develop the well-known *Robert's Rules of Order* after being asked to lead a church meeting that did not go well. There are several forms of guides to parliamentary procedures. *Robert's Rules of Order* is most popular and used by 80% of organizations. Other parliamentary guides include the *Sturgis Standard Code of Parliamentary Procedure*, used especially by physicians and dentists.

The Demeter's Manual of Parliamentary Law and Procedure is used by many labor unions. Other parliamentary books include *Riddick's Rules of Procedure, Mason's Manual of Legislative Procedure* (used by many state legislatures), and *Bourinot's Rules of Order* (used mostly in Canada).

The primary reasons for using parliamentary and other formal procedures are to control the direction of the meeting and to ensure that the meeting or session ends at an appropriate time. It must be made clear, that parliamentary procedure is not about making sure everybody plays fair. Rather, it is about providing a level playing field for all participants. Meetings and sessions without a leader who knows and operates by formalized procedures can get out of control, and extend well beyond a reasonable time frame, often without important matters being resolved or necessary work getting accomplished.

As an investment in yourself, visit the library, bookstore, or log on to the internet where several good parliamentary resources are located. For the beginner, it is better to use a condensed version and learn the basic rules first.

It is also helpful to observe a demonstration of proper parliamentary procedure in action or listen to a certified parliamentarian when the opportunity presents itself.

To hear a parliamentarian, speak or watch a parliamentary demonstration is interesting, and may sound like jargon.

To start, it may be good for a leader to use the simplest and basic form of parliamentary law to help meetings and sessions be as effective, efficient, and productive as possible. Implementing this kind of structure will make a world of a difference.

CHAPTER 4

HOW DO YOU OPERATE?

You have been elected to serve as President of your organization. You have watched the operation for several years, but now the onus for your organizations' success or failure rests squarely on your shoulders. You are concerned that you will not be able to handle the meetings well. You are afraid you may lose control, the business will be conducted poorly, or the meetings may go too long. You have seen some of them go badly under the previous administration. It is also widely known that bad meetings happen very often in the non-profit and community service areas. This happens even when the leader tries to be inclusive, accountable, and well-prepared, which are all necessary ingredients for a good meeting climate.

What words would be used to best describe the meetings? What picture would an artist use to show the quality of the business sessions? How do most of the members feel when they leave the settings that have been planned and facilitated to conduct the organization's business? There should be time taken to determine the answers to these questions as you look at your leadership abilities and how you will make it work.

While looking at the organization's culture and climate, it is a good idea to have a clear understanding of your leadership style and how it fits with this group.

Some established leadership styles include:

- *Autocratic Leaders* – They have total authority to make decisions on their own with no challenges
- *Participative/Democratic Leaders* – They seek input from members, usually in the form of team leaders
- *Coaching Style Leaders* – They groom members through teaching and training
- *Influence Style Leaders* – They use charisma, persuasion, expertise, authority, to lead
- *Transformational Leaders* – They seek to make change happen

In planning to begin a term of leadership or to work to get better, there are some additional areas to be examined closely. Paying attention to these areas will help in facilitating productive and effective meetings.

A. **Know, understand, and own the leader's role in the organization.** If the organization has by-laws, they should clearly define your duties, responsibilities, and powers. In some organizations there are formal and informal roles. The leader and the organization must be clear about what is designated as each officer's responsibilities by the constitution and by-laws, organizational rules, and tradition.

Some general duties of the leader include:

  i) Perform the duties and powers that are assigned to the president or leader.
 ii) Prepare the agenda items for every meeting.
iii) Preside over all meetings of the organization and the Executive Board.
 iv) Ensure that the constitution, by-laws, and established organizational rules are followed.
  v) Appoint all committee chairpersons and assist them in carrying out their duties if needed.

vi) Sign checks and the appropriate documents and confer with the Treasurer on all checks and financial obligations of the organization as needed.

vii) Set, adhere to, and enforce deadlines.

viii) Serve as the main point of contact for the organization.

B. **Plan the agenda carefully.** A well-planned agenda is the first step in ensuring that the meeting does not go awry.

i) *Set the agenda in advance.* Ask the Executive Board and committee chairpersons for agenda items at least a week before the meeting. This allows them to have time to prepare well for any proposal or event on which they need to report.

ii) *Combine all agenda items and send the complete agenda out prior to the meeting in order to receive any necessary feedback.* If there are items that may require a large amount of deliberation, it is good to go over these with Board members and iron out as many of the potential problems as possible.

iii) *Prepare people to speak to these topics.* They should do their research, prepare a presentation if needed, bring handouts, and be ready to speak to the issue or answer any questions. It is important not to waste people's time.

iv) *Appoint a timekeeper and note taker.* Start on time and stick to allotted times as much as possible. Value your members time and resources. Use the agenda to organize notes that can be easily accessed during the meeting and before official minutes are distributed.

C. **Oversee the logistics of the meeting location.** The effective leader must know more than the group's decision-making process to make sure the meeting will go well. Eliminating logistical problems is important and requires attention to details. The president who has everyone waiting for half an hour because someone forgot to mention that there is a need for an appropriate connector cord for the important presentation will have someone leave the meeting in a bad mood. Even if someone must run out and buy one it is an imposition.

If a PowerPoint presentation is being shown, have it saved in several formats (PC, Mac, and PDF are examples). Order, confirm, and collect all AV equipment, laptops, and connector cords that will be needed. Check that markers work, and that flip chart paper and /or whiteboards are available for use.

Make sure the room is appropriate and as comfortable as possible. Meetings should take place in a quiet place that allows appropriate discussion and movement.

Arrive about 30 minutes early to ensure that everything is in place as needed to keep the meeting flowing smoothly.

Plan for refreshments or breaks for meetings that last more than 90 minutes.

Respect the Culture and the Codes

Successful and productive meetings and programs require more than just knowing a group's decision-making processes. Each group has its own unique way of operating and managing its meetings. Organizational meeting cultures vary, and the astute leader learns as many of the unique differences as possible before beginning.

BusinessDictionary.com defines organizational culture as, "The values and behaviors that contribute to the unique social and psychological environment of an organization." It also points out that organizational culture may include an organization's expectations, experiences, philosophy, and values that hold it together.

These are expressed in its self-image, inner workings, interactions with the outside world, and future expectations. The developed culture is based on shared attitude related experiences, beliefs, customs, and written and unwritten rules that have been established during the lifetime of the organization and are considered valid.

Also included in organizational culture is a system of shared assumptions, values, and beliefs that determines the behavior of members in an organization. These are usually old and established values that have maintained a strong influence on the people in the organization. New organizations usually begin to develop cultural modes immediately. Every organization develops and maintains its own specific culture.

The developed culture sets the guidelines and boundaries for members' behavior, how they dress, who works together, how meetings will be conducted, and how the organization will flow, for example.

In large measure, organizational culture is composed of characteristics that can be identified and given varying levels of priority. Some characteristics are:

1. **Attending to Details**- Organizations that spend a lot of time on process, precision, rituals, and dress codes fall into this category. Those that place a high value on this characteristic are not as concerned with positive productivity as they are with how they are perceived in public.

2. **Emphasis on Outcomes** - Results are the focus for organizations that place a high value on this characteristic. When the leaders do not care how the results are attained or who gets offended or hurt in the process, it is indicative of too much high value being placed on this characteristic.

3. **Collaborating as Teams** – Organizations that organize the work of the body around teams and identified groups rather than individuals place a high value on this organizational culture. There may be many factors that influence how the teams are chosen, who works with whom, who provides the leadership, and what work is done by whom. However, people who are involved in this type of culture must have positive relationships with other members and the leadership.

4. **Innovative Atmosphere** – Some organizational leaders encourage the members to be innovative in their planning and facilitating of the organization's activities. This high-risk culture has value because it allows members to be creative and move into new areas without fear. Organizations that place a low value on innovation expect their members to do their jobs and assignments the same way they have been doing them for years without a rationale. They are not encouraged to look for new and better ways that might improve their organization or themselves.

While useful in some organization cultures, it can create a stagnant climate that does not grow easily.

5. **Secure Stability** – Organizations that place a high value on stability are rule-conscious, predictable, and often operate in a bureaucratic manner.

   They usually are consistent and predictable in their performance whether it is good or bad. They like to be able to forecast with authority what the results of most actions will be.

6. **People Oriented** – This characteristic in the organizational culture is best described as one which places a great deal of value on how the processes and decision making will affect the people in the membership. In these organizations all people are treated with respect and afforded dignity. Many feel that this characteristic adds to the longevity and viability of some organizations.

7. **Assertive Competitiveness** – Some organizations develop a culture where members are aggressively competitive when dealing with other groups or individuals.

It is important to them to be seen as number one in their arena. These types of organizations place a high value on being competitive and outperforming the competition. In many cases, they want to win no matter what the consequences or costs may be.

The astute leader studies the organization's culture which will determine in large measure the guidelines for the leadership provided and how it will work. For example, it may influence how much the members are willing to work to obtain the productivity desired, how members treat each other, attendance and punctuality, interactions with outside agencies and organizations, and concern for the organization.

CHAPTER 5

SETTING MANAGEMENT GOALS

The late Dr. C. A. Kirkendoll, Sr. former President of Lane College, Bishop of the Christian Methodist Episcopal Church, and noted educator and preacher, stood in the pulpit of the Lane College Chapel. He was preaching to the congregation of mostly students and faculty about the value of institutional and community ownership for what had transpired on the college campus during one night in the tumultuous 70's. He said,

> Let me tell you a story that stays with me. A little child about two years old tries to cross the street and is hit by a car in the middle of the street. The child lays there helplessly face down as the crowd gathers around. Someone had called the police, so they heard the sirens going off as the police rushed to the scene. A woman in her home looked out the window and ran out to the injured child. She picked the child up, gathered it tenderly in her arms, and caressed it as she held it to her breast. After a moment, she moved the child back to examine the injuries. She looked at the toddler and said, "This is not my child." And she put the child back down in the street and went back into her house.

Most of us have seen floundering organizations that could benefit individuals and the community with just a little help, but many times we said, "This is not my child." However, when the leadership falls on your shoulders, everybody's help is wanted and needed. You want everybody to claim and help the child. But often deciding on the management of the organization is an individual, one-person task.

Effective leaders set reachable management goals for the organization. Management goals provide focus on the steps needed for everyone in the organization to work cooperatively and push the organization to higher levels of success. Much of the organizational management style of today's organizations of color comes from the Black church which is an organization that has maintained an enormous presence in most communities throughout history.

Dr. Marvin Andrew McMickie, President and Professor of Church Leadership of *Colgate Rochester Crozer Divinity School,* Rochester, NY, in an *Encyclopedia of African American Christian Heritage* writes about the role of the Black church in America.

According to McMickie, the African American church has had a grave impact. He says:

> ...this institution was the first source of land ownership for slaves in America. In African American history 'the church' has been the epicenter of the Black community. It has established itself as the greatest source for African American religious enrichment but also took much of the responsibility for the early management of educational, social, and political development as well.

In his classic, *The History of the Negro Church* Carter G. Woodson traces the influence of the Black church in America from colonial times through the early years of the twentieth century. After the Civil war, Woodson says the church took on a new more important role as an organizational base and meeting place for social and political activities, and centers for economic development and growth.

It is from this organizational structure that most of the organizations of color took their management styles. They developed, implementing the management strategies that were good and solid as well as those that had no real value to the organization. ***Today's successful organizational leaders continue to use that which is useful but recognize the need to maximize all opportunities for the organization by also utilizing current management strategies.***

Financial Acumen and Management

Most people who did not major in business have little knowledge of how to account for the money that comes into the organizations they lead. Usually organization leaders understand the importance of mission achievement through appropriate programs and are trained in delivering services. But, leaders and managers of organizations of color should develop at least basic skills in financial management. When it is expected that others in the organization will manage the finances while you know nothing, you are asking for trouble real fast. Sometimes leaders set themselves up for failure in the financial arena because they view it as something too hard for them to learn or they simply lack skill and desire.

Dr. Sharron Taylor Burnett, currently Executive Vice President and Chief Financial Officer, Tuskegee University, describes it this way: "In a way, finance is much like technology to some people. They are afraid of it, but also feel they are entitled to be exempt from learning anything about the numbers." She says further, "Even the word 'finance' is intimidating to many people.

She continues:

> *Most would rather think about the mission and the programs rather than the financial plan. The challenge and opportunity for the leader is to learn how to make the numbers meaningful even to the members whose background is not finance. There must also be the understanding that strategic planning requires the integration of mission, programs, and financial planning. They must be in alignment if the organization is to be successful.*

Historically, much of today's financial management strategies were borrowed from the church and other community groups that allowed one person to serve as the Chief Financial Officer. This person usually served as the Treasurer, Secretary, and in any other position that dealt with fiduciary matters.

Basic skills in financial management start in the critical areas of cash management and bookkeeping. These should be done according to certain financial controls to ensure integrity in the money management and bookkeeping process. The leader should get the appropriate training to learn how to generate financial statements and analyze them to really understand the financial condition of the organization.

Nonprofit Accounting Basics.org lists a cycle of four good management habits whether the organization is large or small.

Sound procedures and internal controls help ensure accurate accounting and high-quality reporting.

Evaluation of the information included in the report assists in the planning, development, and facilitation of organizational programming. Program development and financial management can be improved by consistent evaluation of the financial processes.

Components of the Financial Management Cycle

1. **Basics and Getting Started** – Review the basics of non-profit financial management. Or if your national body has an accounting system, ensure that you are aligned with and follow their guidelines:

   - What type of bookkeeping system will be used?
   - Will you use a software package to automate your financial management?
   - Get to know your bank and a banker.
   - Address financial controls and risk management.

2. **Budgeting and Financial Planning** – Financial planning will require that you spend some time with your Financial Officers and Board members providing financial oversight for the organization:

   - Develop an annual operating budget with financial committee and Board.
   - Have the budget approved as mandated by organizational guidelines.
   - Monitor the organization's adherence to the budget.
   - Set long range goals and funding strategies for achieving them.

3. **Reporting**– Effective finance committees provide financial reports that clearly articulate the organization's financial and cash position:

   - Develop financial report formats that are useful, readable, and understandable.
   - Determine the list of reports to be prepared.
   - Set timelines for presenting the reports to the membership.

4. **Internal Controls and Accountability Policies** – Internal controls are financial practices that are used to prevent misuse and misappropriations of assets. They are usually a part of written policies that tells what procedure is to be followed, as well as who is responsible for what. The goal of established internal controls is to create business practices that serve as "checks and balances". This is important with large corporations and even with smaller non-profit organizations. The following controls that are workable for most organizations are suggested as follows:

- High priority should be given to setting an environment in which everyone knows that policies are in place and they are to be followed by everyone starting with the top. This climate of control will help to eliminate sloppy or unethical tones that lead to irresponsible behaviors.

- Clearly define and state who has responsibility for what. In many organizations it is common not to write a lot down. But the more that is stated is better for the organization in the long run.

  For example, "There will be two signatures on every check." "The

Secretary will check the math on the invoice and pass it to the Treasurer for payment." "Reimbursements will only be made for expenses that were approved in writing in advance."

- When cash is handled, i.e., a fundraiser, have two people count and record the amount of the money together.

- A critical point in the financial picture is reconciling the bank statement. Ideally someone other than the person who handles the money should reconcile the bank account directly from an unopened statement.

- Physical Control can be a pivotal point in the process of establishing accountability. If the organization has an office this is paramount. Organization property should be locked up with a written policy on who has access. Checks should be kept in a locked drawer or file cabinet. Among other abuses, there are cases where people came in and took checks from the middle of the checkbook. Computers should be protected with organization passwords.

In even the smallest organization, there can be another person who periodically looks over things or audits the books. The audit ensures that all is well within the organization's financial realm, or not. Often financial officers resist the idea of the books being audited. It is viewed as an accusation of stealing or mishandling the funds. The audit is a safeguard for the organization, and should be performed annually, preferably by a professional.

DEVELOPING DIFFERENTIATED MANAGEMENT STRATEGIES TO MEET ORGANIZATIONAL OBJECTIVES

The decision about the road one takes is very often made by knowing the destination at which one wishes to be at the end of the journey. The best leaders of organizations spend much time in defining the organizational vision and planning how to make it a reality. Therefore, they have a better idea of the roads to take to complete the organizational journey.

Dr. Vickie Cox Edmondson, an academic and management strategist who has taught strategic management to graduating business students for more than 25 years, emphasizes the importance of crafting strategies tied to *S.M.A.R.T* performance objectives in her book, *The Thinking Strategist: Unleashing the Power of Strategic Management to Identify, Explore, and Solve Problems.* As shown in this figure, *S.M.A.R.T.* is an acronym for:

- Specific
- Measurable
- Attainable
- Relevant
- Timely

Figure 2 S.M.A.R.T TRIANGLE

Organizational strategies may be defined as the actions and benchmarks an organization puts in place to ensure that long-term goals and objectives are achieved. These plans list the steps in a sequence that must be completed to make the idea a reality. It must be kept in mind that this process is a marathon, not a sprint. This process requires extreme oversight into every aspect of the organization's operations and an understanding of the main audiences to which the organization will appeal.

Well-developed organizational strategies are essential for achieving long-term goals and the ongoing success of the enterprise. The organizational strategy should determine the outcome that is desired and provide a plan for making it happen. During the process, there should be a comparison of current circumstances with overall objectives. Areas in need of improvement should be isolated. A method to change the areas in need of improvement should be formulated in order to better achieve the organization's stated goals. Likewise, be mindful of things that are working well. Call attention to people, processes, and projects that are serving the organization well. This often increases the success of your strategy.

As strategies are being developed it is important to choose or revise the organization's core values. Remember, one must serve the present age and time in which the organization exists.

Innovation can often make a visible and valuable difference. Dare to be different. Be creative in your planning. Often it is found that needs are served better when we leave the beaten path. As with any move that is different and involves other people, be aware that things will not always work as planned.

Be patient. A solid organizational strategy that leads to a competitive brand is most often built by hard work and persistence.

Creating a differentiation strategy allows the organization to focus on its most important parts in its planning and operations and keeps everyone on the same page. The strategy can also reduce confusion between leaders so that the teams are able to function as one. This provides a means for directing their efforts in a more productive manner. Organizational strategies lead to generating directives that are aimed at producing positive long-term goals.

Differentiation essentially means making your organization or brand stand out by identifying the unique features, benefits, services, or other elements that make it unique. This strategy means identifying the important criteria being sought and designing the programs and projects in ways that best meet those needs. A differentiation strategy calls for creating or identifying sufficiently distinctive attributes within the organization that sets it apart from the rest.

It is the leader's responsibility to ensure that no matter what the current practice, process, or strategy is, the integrity of the organization is always maintained. There should never be any wavering when the questions from within or without are raised, "Who are we?" and "What are we about?"

To ensure that the organization runs smoothly, effectively, and as intended the leader must make certain there is structure in place. Organizational structure is something that is best decided upon through internal collaboration, using a process of critical thinking and open discussion by members. The structure development or review discussion should be a part of the early planning.

Some questions that may be considered in the discussions that may guide your decisions include:

1. What is your common purpose?
2. Are you a group that advocates or provides services? If your group has a broad purpose it will have a more complicated and complex structure. These organizations require several layers and parts to operate effectively. Groups with more narrow purposes can have much simpler purposes.
3. Are you a locally centralized group? Or are you a part of a national organization?
4. How large is your organization? How large do you envision it becoming?
5. How large is the community in which your organization is located?
6. Is your organization new or is it a part of an already existing structure?
7. Is your organization comprised strictly of volunteers, or are there (will there be) paid staff?
8. In the end, for what would you like to be remembered? As an individual? As a group?

CHAPTER 6

FINDING, DEVELOPING AND KEEPING THE RIGHT PEOPLE

A major goal of most organizations is to have an active and robust membership of high-quality people in the right positions and a culture that keeps them excited about being there. Today's leaders must keep in mind that the organization must maintain enough viability that it is appealing enough to attract and retain the younger millennials or the upcoming *Generation Z.*

Historically, organizations of color were small and individual members had to fill several roles to ensure the success of the organization. Often a member of the organization would develop a certain skill set because it was needed and there was no one else able to do the task. In addition, there was usually a great deal of support given as this process evolved.

Everybody worked to help their colleagues be at their best no matter what the assignment. This cultural characteristic that was born out of necessity is one of the elements that make for winning teams.

Continuing in this vein, today's leaders must ensure that recruiting strategies and individual assessments improve the chances of getting the right people to your front door or maintaining and growing the current membership. This concept can be equated with building a solid 'bench'. Winning teams have a starting line-up, but they are aware that they need a strong bench in case a starter or the entire starting team needs to come out of the game. In the same way, know the starters, but have a clear picture of what the bench looks like, just in case.

Tony Dungy can be described as a successful coach and leader. As the coach of the *Indianapolis Colts*, of the National Football League, he led the team to the Super Bowl and captured the win. In his book, *The Mentor Leader*, Dungy states that being a mentor and developing your people is a crucial part of leadership. He says, "Building a life of significance and creating a legacy of real value means being willing to get your hands dirty."

This means that the organizational leader must get to know the people who make up the membership.

The implication also is that provisions must be made to ensure that someone is prepared to take on any task that might be presented. According to Dungy, the leader may have to take responsibility for some things that are not in the current job description.

Define the primary abilities and character traits that the organization needs and watch for them in the current membership or when looking for new members. This is usually a two-fold process. The astute leader is always conscious of the present membership and the possibilities of assisting them in expanding their reach. At the same time, the leader must be aware that new members can offer the opportunity to fill some ability cracks if they exist. Putting the two together in a cohesive manner can create a well-oiled organizational machine.

Seek people to put out front who can motivate others and create a warm and welcoming environment. In his book, *The Secrets of Success*, Eric Thomas, also known as ET, the Hip Hop Preacher, writes about the principles of leadership. Principle Number Eight is: "The right environment is pivotal to your success." It is also crucial to the success of your members.

The relational connection between what the organization looks and feels like and the engagement of the members is astounding. Cultivate a winning environment.

Attracting and maintaining members is much like growing crops. We can make this analogy because we watched our dad and granddad, an incredibly smart man, as he worked hard to make a living from the good earth. We learned that the quality of the ground into which the seeds were planted impacted the level of productivity of the crop. The climate or atmosphere is important in crop growth. Some grow better when it is hot, and others flourish in cooler weather. That says to the leader that there needs to be an understanding of the temperament and personality of each member and the development of an environment in which each can grow.

John C. Maxwell, an expert in leadership principles and team building, lists five levels in his early book called *Developing the Leader in You.* Level Four speaks to people development and production. According to Maxwell a leader empowers followers and helps them grow personally.

It is his theory that people follow because of loyalty brought about by how the leader has helped them grow. Maxwell lists the following indicators of excellence in this area:

A. Recognizes people are valuable assets
B. Role models for others to follow
C. Develops people
D. Shares goals
E. Surround oneself with a core group that complements the leadership philosophy
F. Leadership is coursed through the core group

It does not matter how long the coach played, how much expertise she has about the game, or how much she knows about the other team, there will not be many wins unless she has a winning team. Winning teams usually are made up of members with a variety of talents. These individuals know how to play several different roles or positions as a part of the team. The coach tries to ensure that everybody recognizes and appreciates the different abilities and strengths that each member brings to the team. The coach knows how to help the team members blend their talents to work well together and help one another.

Individuals who have a wide range of talents, who can play diverse roles within the team, and who respect each other usually make winning teams. Everybody recognizes and appreciates the different strengths of each member on winning teams. This means that one stops thinking about those things that make us different and are reasons to label us as superior or inferior to one another.

It is important to remember that good leaders are good at producing more leaders, not just members who follow them. This concept influences who is brought into the organization or company and how they are prepared for the next level.

CHAPTER 7

EXTERNAL LINKS

In today's fast paced world, organizations that wish to be successful and grow are looking for more than technical expertise, in-depth job knowledge, or the ability to get along with each other. They are seeking leaders who understand techniques for engaging people, processes, and policies often with people who do not belong to the same organization. Leaders of organizations of color must be particularly astute as they seek to navigate the invisible but powerful cultural forces before them as they work for the good of their organizations. The crooked paths of the external links can often make or break a leader.

Often leading the organization will require the development of external interactions, negotiations, and relationships.

The quality and extent of external interactions are sometimes determined by the desired result of the forces being joined. Both parties should be clear regarding the expected outcomes if there are any. *Some external interactions are entered for the benefit of your organization while others may be for the greater good.* As a leader you should have clarity about the expectations of all the entities that are involved, an action plan, resources needed, and how you will determine the worth of the interaction. Negotiation and collaboration skills are important for the best leaders when dealing with other organizations and agencies.

Collaborative Leadership

Collaboration is working together to get an identified task completed. Interaction among several groups and individuals is often needed to address complex or group related issues. The use of collaboration requires shared interest leadership.

In using collaboration, it is important to remember that it is the results of the combined efforts of the alliance that count.

It is easy to get hung up on who will get the credit or whose name will be called first.

However, the real questions revolve around how one can be sure to take care of the problem for the benefit of all. Turning back to the game of chess, the rook has the lowest point value in the game. As mentioned previously, the rook is the foot soldier and is always the first to fall. As the leader of your organization, you will need to make sure that your group is not being positioned to be the rook, doing the hard work only to be pushed aside at the end. And before you think to use another person or organization in this manner, consider if the consequences are worth it. You could lose the trust of all other groups and gain a less than desirable reputation for yourself and your organization.

Collaborative leadership is best defined as a process, rather than what the leaders do and who they are. In this kind of cooperative leadership there are many similarities to servant leadership and transformational leadership.

According to David Chrislip and Carl Lawson in *Collaborative Leadership*, "if you bring the right people together in constructive ways with good information, they will create authentic visions and strategies for addressing the shared concerns of the organization or community."

Collaborative leadership may be practiced as an internal function among leaders of one organization or by several organizations working together for the same purpose. However, it is seen most often in community coalitions and initiatives.

Organizational success often depends on having good collaborative working relations with a wide range of individuals and organizations. These may include:

- Other Boards
- Governmental Agencies
- Business Owners and Management
- Funding Agencies
- Professionals in Other Fields
- Political Groups
- Colleges and Universities

Principled Negotiations

The skill of negotiating is important to anyone who is in or seeks a leadership position. This skill is used today in almost everything from "where will we meet?" to "how much will the budget be?"

Fisher and Ury caution that negotiation is not a matter of butting heads and making concessions to get the job done. In their book, *Getting to Yes*, they see principled negotiations as best for most organizations- deciding issues on their merits. They discourage bargaining over positions, people, and other items that do not affect the value or quality of the decision to be made. In these cases, it is likely that all will get locked down and sidetracked from meeting the concerns of any of the parties. Agreement is usually less likely in these circumstances.

Doing appropriate homework is a vital part of the negotiation process. Never lose sight of the fact that agreements are reached because both sides see some benefits for them. Therefore, one should be well prepared prior to beginning the negotiations.

Below are necessary steps:

- **Do the appropriate research**. Gather all the information that is available that may have bearing on the case to be presented.
- **Know the other side.** Know what is important to the adversary or the agency from which the favor is being sought. What are the likes and dislikes?

Do not be narrow-minded. Learn about the other side's degree of flexibility.

- **Plan your strategy.** What will it take to get the results wanted? What will happen if the requests are met? Who will be on the team?
  What are the consequences if the other side wins? How, when, and where, will the negotiations be scheduled?

- **Rehearse each step.** Spend some time going over the steps in the negotiations. Use another sound thinking person who will be a challenger and play the devil's advocate. Be sure to be well prepared before entering the arena.

- **Enter the arena confidently.** Do enough homework to know the importance of the impending discussions. Walk into the room as if you know your value and the value of the product or concept that you will present. There is only one opportunity to make a good first impression. Take advantage of each one.

Organizational Relationships and Partnerships

When leading a group, it is often necessary to develop relationships with other organizations in order to reach the identified goals and objectives you have established.

Organizations can often find additional strength in building alliances with other organizations that share similar goals. However, it must be kept in mind that even organizations with similar goals are likely to have differing perspectives, experiences, needs, and desires for the relationship or partnership.

It is important for all involved to jointly develop plans that maximize the unique contributions that each one brings to the table in order to create a smooth and coordinated working relationship.

The development of relationships in an organization and partnerships with other entities can be a pivotal movement for the leader. Research shows that organizational relationship management theory is a relatively new paradigm. But understanding and managing the relationships can have value to the individual, the organization, and the greater society.

When contacting an organization about working together on a project or developing a partnership, consider all the factors necessary for a solid relationship. While the most pressing concern may be facilitating your event, consider the needs and wants of the other party.

Some questions to ask when seeking to build a relationship with another organization include:

- Partnerships require more time from both parties. Is your organization in a position to give the needed time to make it work?
- Are there any foreseeable risks that might be encountered by working with this organization?
- Have the organization's intentions been communicated clearly to the organization/agency?
- Has consideration been given to how this relationship might add to or complicate your organization's agenda that is already planned?
- Will this be a reciprocal relationship/partnership in which all parties understand and support the other's goals?
- Are all parties' opinions respected?

One of the largest pieces that leaders must put into relationship building is trust. Developing trust within an organizational relationship or partnership is crucial to its success.

Developing trust will often require time and resources to ensure a process that will ultimately improve all parties that are involved.

General Colin Powell, former Secretary of State, talks about trust and leadership in his book, *It Worked for Me in Life and Leadership*.

He says, "Leadership is solving problems. The day soldiers stop bringing you their problems you have stopped leading them. They have either lost confidence that you can help or concluded that you do not care. Either case is a failure of leadership." The same is true for organizational relationships. When the talking stops, the partnership has often died.

Building relationships or partnering with others can provide a great deal of strength and diversity. But it can also pose an organizational challenge. The leaders must ensure that an efficient process is designed that will promote effective communication, planning, and coordination. All parties should feel important to the team. No one should take the position that we are "helping them" through this collaboration.

CHAPTER 8

THE ROLE OF INFORMATION TECHNOLOGY

A wise man adapts himself to circumstances, as water shapes itself to the vessel that contains it. This Chinese proverb speaks to many organizations of color who reluctantly face the age of information technology. However, even smaller organizations need to use some information technology to increase efficiency and to save time and money. Today information technology has presented us with many opportunities to streamline our operations. Let us take a simple example. In the past, organizations had to mostly use direct mail or phone calls to reach the membership. But today all it takes is a well-crafted email which is only sent once, and all the members are informed. However, do not forget to keep the senior members and others who are not computer literate informed about organizational matters.

In speaking about the necessity to change with the times Charles Darwin said, "It is not the strongest or most intelligent who will survive, but those who can best manage change." Information technology provides wonderful and exciting ways to promote organizational growth and sustainability through change. The organizations that move to the use of information technology will usually have a longer and more productive life span.

With information technology, organizations do not have to spend as much money on papers and expensive means to store data and files. Now the organization can create an internal database which records and keeps this information. A good thing is that this database can be updated as needed to meet specific requirements.

Information technology is a much cheaper way to market and reach target audiences. In the past, organizational business, membership development, and internal and external surveys were a large part of the organization's budget and time resources. Organizations can now get data about their membership, potential members, and other targeted groups by using internet cookies and web surveys.

Communication can be simplified for all concerned by information technology. The use of technologies such as the fax machine, email, and e-commerce open doors to many areas of organizational advancement and growth. They save time and money.

Another example of organizational use of information technology is for telephone or video conferencing. The utilizing of this technology allows meetings to be held, presentations to be made, and products to be advertised and sold without members being present.

With the increased use of social media, many organizations are embracing this technology by communicating with targeted audiences directly in an entertainment and informational manner. An organization can start a Facebook page for free and they can use it to interact with members, clients, and others. A Facebook page can be created free today and linked to your organization's web sites or your offline advertising. This will cause many people to look at your Facebook page, as well as other social media tools.

When organizations use information technology security issues must become a concern. It can become central to how the organization operates.

Networks and computers may hold data on membership, finances, organizational secrets, and personal information.

This is data which the organization has a legal obligation to protect. The organization's leadership must ensure that there is not too much access to the data so there will not be a breach of security. However, no one person should have all access or unmonitored access to important data and systems.

When resisting this change, remember the words of Kauzo OKakaura, Japanese scholar and noted art critic, "The art of living is a constant readjustment to our surroundings." Information technology is making us change and readjust, but it is worth it to the leader and the organization.

CHAPTER 9

HOW DID WE DO? SELF-ASSESSMENT

There comes a time in all phases of organizational life when it is expedient to step back and ask a few questions. Some examples that can be used are: Where are we today? How far have we come? Did we get here in the best possible way? What does tomorrow look like as we project? Will we survive tomorrow? These are examples of questions that are raised when thinking about organizational evaluation.

Organizational evaluation results can have a wide array of uses. For example, they may be used by an organization to help build its capacity, to assess the value of its programs and projects, to establish or expand its brand, to determine member satisfaction, to promote dialog with funders or partners, and to help in planning for future operations.

Evaluation is an important tool for leaders to use to determine the health and efficiency of the organization. However, it must be kept in mind that Albert Einstein, noted physicist, said, "Everything that can be counted does not necessarily count; everything that counts cannot necessarily be counted." Another quote by Peter Drucker, management consultant, educator, and author, that has bearing on the evaluation process and how it will be used is, "The most serious mistakes are not being made as a result of wrong answers. The most dangerous thing is asking the wrong questions." Through organizational assessment or evaluation that asks the right questions, the effectiveness of the organization is measured in terms of its functioning, problem solving, and achievements. It can play an important role in helping leaders improve the efficiency and effectiveness of their operations and can be instruments for creating public trust in the outreach activities.

Some organizations never do real and meaningful evaluations. Some of the reason's leaders give for excluding this process include:

- **I am not sure how we should do this...**
  Most of us did not know at some point, so that is a fair statement. But you and members who have these abilities and want to grow can learn how to do it. Many organizations are connected to National Offices that have evaluation processes already in place.
- **I am too busy with the programs to do that now...**
  The programs and outreach are the heart and soul of most organizations. So, it is natural to spend a lot of time in their execution. But it is necessary to stop and see if the organization is facilitating them effectively and that the established goals were set.
- **It will cost too much...**
  Connect with people in the industry and get as much free and reliable guidance as possible. Use all the community resources in this area that are available.
- **What we do cannot be measured...**
  If the planned programs are very vague and have goals and objectives that are not well stated and measurable it may be difficult to make meaning of the evaluation.
- **I just know we are doing a good job...**
  Sometimes the gut or intuition may not be the best measuring stick.

Sometimes a solid evaluation will call attention to issues that were not a part of the intuitive scene. Real evaluation takes the organization to accountability places that the gut does not know exists.

- **I do not see why it matters...**
  Evaluation is the only real way to determine if the organization is doing what had been planned to do and to judge the value of that work. It also ensures that the recommendations are realistic and feasible.

- **I am afraid of what I might find out...**
  The fear is understandable. But what is scarier is what might be going on that you might not find without appropriate evaluations.

- **All of this does not prove anything anyway...**
  Just as with most measurements one cannot show 100% proof that everything done was effective. But evidence can be gathered that shows the role the organization   played and document some of the results of the members' participation.

Why Do Organizations Need Evaluation?

Over the past several years, many organizations of color have become more interested in strengthening their management and governance.

Development activities such as leadership development, strategic planning, program design and development, Board development, and evaluation methods are becoming a regular part of programmatic planning. Research is showing that investing in organizational capacity building helps leverage the impact of the resources that are available to them. The questions then are raised, "What makes an organization effective?", "How and why do we evaluate?", "And then what?"

Evaluation has several purposes contingent upon where the organization is in its development and what the leadership wishes to ascertain from the process. One of the major goals of evaluation is to determine organizational effectiveness. *Many evaluators define effectiveness in terms of how well the organization accomplishes its goals.* Business Dictionary.Com defines organizational effectiveness as: The efficiency and effectiveness with which an organization can meet its goals and objectives. Inherent in the definition is the degree to which they are being met for organizations of color.

A rational view of effectiveness focuses on ensuring that goals are attained and the quality and quantity of the productivity.

Some measures of this effectiveness may be expressed in terms of how the projected membership growth compares with actual membership growth. Additional measures can include results from membership satisfaction surveys, program productivity, member turnover, organizational stability and standing in the community, and financial status and growth.

The social system of determining effectiveness will emphasize more people-oriented functions such as membership satisfaction, morale, interpersonal relations, and community view of the organization.

A second approach to evaluation is to check accountability. A statement that we have heard for a long time and do not know to whom to give the credit for saying it is "You either hold yourself accountable or you will be made accountable by your circumstances." Dr. Verda Farrow, retired teacher and administrator in the Broward County, Florida School District, often spoke about the area of personal and organizational accountability.

She says that, "Hell begins the day when you face God and he lets you see clearly all that you might have achieved, all the gifts you have wasted, and all that you might have done with what he gave you which you did not do."

That is called personal accountability. It is not very pleasant when colleagues and members can see that things promised were not delivered because the leader has not been accountable.

In organizations where leaders and members agree on what is to be done, follow through to ensure that it is done well, keep their commitment to the product, and deliver what is promised, accountability never needs to be formally viewed. But sometimes is made available for others to review.

Making the change to a culture of organizational accountability begins with assessing and reviewing the current culture as it is seen from everyday behaviors. It is necessary to acknowledge and confront the behaviors and activities that are not measuring up to the set standards. There must be clarity about the definitions of the desired practices. Identify both leadership and member behaviors that are the desired practices. If changes need to be made, put the whole group on notice. Develop together a clear vision and consistent message about the direction in which the organization will move.

When the need arises some questions to be raised include:

- Who is responsible for what in the area we are examining now?
- Should some practices or processes be changed?
- Would different people in strategic places make a difference?
- Is it a leadership or membership issue?
- Does a major change need to take place?
- Is the vision clear to all parties?

Some intervention strategies can now be put into place. Start with the issues that are easiest to fix. Be sure there is a clear understanding of the expected organizational culture and then hold everyone accountable.

A third reason for evaluation is to determine ways to make improvements. *While evaluations and assessments have many purposes one that should always be in the forefront is how to take what is learned and make the organization better.* To do this the purpose and intent of the assessment should be clear to the members and stakeholders. The focus should be on learning rather than placing blame. The tools and resources necessary to support any suggested change should be in place.

A fourth approach focuses on the effectiveness of the internal procedures and operations of the organization. Other areas that can be assessed include Organizational Health, Organizational Effectiveness, and Organization Sustainability. For a more in-depth assessment, organization leaders may examine organizational capacity to include:

- Program management
- Process Management
- Financial Management
- Inter-organizational Relationships
- Leadership Development Strategies, Infrastructure
- Management Structure
- Human Resources

An evaluation of Organizational Performance usually includes the effectiveness of the programming, the efficiency with which matters are handled, financial stability, and the relevance of current activities. The External Environment plays a role in how well an organization functions and should be reviewed to determine the extent to which it positively or negatively affects the working of the organization.

This may include Administrative Constraints, Political, Economic, Technological Issues, Stakeholders, Community Cultural Barriers, and Legal Parameters. The results of organizational assessment can have a wide variety of uses.

For example, they can be used to help an organization determine and build its capacity, validate its programming and work, promote and document conversation with partners and funders, and help plan.

The size, complexity, history, mission, and culture of the community and the organization will help in determining the degree of evaluation and assessment that will be used.

Moreover, high impact leaders do not spend a lot of time looking back on past errors and wasted time. They do not wallow in past mistakes and allow them to become the measuring stick for who or what they can become.

CHAPTER 10

HONORING THE PARLIAMENTARY RULES

Any meeting will run more smoothly when the leader knows and ensures parliamentary procedure is being followed. According to *Robert's Rules of Order Parliamentary* procedure is simply a standard set of rules used to conduct business meetings. When set rules are used for each meeting and each issue, participants know what to expect and have a clear opportunity to voice their opinions and vote in an orderly manner. While organizations are not required to follow Robert's Rules, it is good to abide by them during the decision-making processes of the meeting. A good leader helps the membership know and understand the value of having rules and structure.

Some common decision-making structures that can help meeting flow include:

- *Consensus:* Everyone agrees, or everyone agrees not to oppose an issue.
- *Majority vote:* The decision is approved by most of the members present.
- *Quorum:* A quorum is the minimum number of members who must be present for the meeting to be conducted. The quorum is usually based on a percentage or fraction of the members and is usually established in advance.
- *Order of the Day:* Order of the Day is simply how the meeting is presented and what business will be conducted at this session. Each meeting should have its own agenda that includes issues to be discussed, reports to be made, old business, and new business to be considered. It helps the decision-making process if each attendee has a copy of the agenda.
- *Making a motion:* One important principle in parliamentary procedure is the process of making and voting on motions. All business should be decided by a motion and a vote by the members present.

There are five simple steps for making a motion that provide basic language that will usually work at most meeting settings. We list this below:

1. **Get Recognized** - It is important that a member of the organization first have the floor (get recognized) before presenting a motion or a new order of business. This is typically done simply by the raising of a hand or addressing the presiding officer. The presiding officer will then acknowledge or recognize the member.

2. **Motion is presented** – The proper language the maker of the motion should use is, "I move that we..." An example of the correct language is simply, "I move that we do a campus clean-up for our community service project next month." The complete intention should be stated in the motion.

3. **Motion is seconded** – The proper language is, "I second the motion." "Support" is commonly used, but it is improper language. Seconding a motion may simply mean that the individual wants to move the item to the floor for discussion. The second is not necessarily an indication of support for the motion.

4. **Motion is discussed** – The opportunity for the members to discuss the motion should only come after it has been properly brought to the floor by being moved and seconded.

A common mistake in many meetings is that many ideas are discussed at length before the issue is presented in the form of a motion.

While discussion is often needed to provide clarity, intent, or better understanding of the concept, it should only come after the motion has been properly put on the floor by a motion and a second. Motions that are properly made and seconded are considered active. The moderator of the meeting will open the floor for discussion. Participants who wish to speak should indicate they want to be recognized and wait for the moderator to call on them. This keeps discussion orderly and reduces members interrupting each other and talking over one another. Discussion can continue for as long as needed. But the leader should keep it orderly, as brief as possible, and to the issue at hand.

5. **Vote is taken on the motion** – After an appropriate period of discussion, the president or chairperson should call for a vote on the motion that is on the floor. Voting can be conducted in several ways. The method by which the vote will be taken should be established in advance. Voting can be conducted in several ways, a voice vote ("aye" or "nay"), by the raising of hands, by roll call, or by secret ballot.

Motions that are properly made and seconded are considered active. The moderator of the meeting will open the floor for discussion.

Participants who wish to speak should indicate they want to be recognized and wait for the moderator to be recognized.

It should be noted that Robert's rules are designed to facilitate the conducting of business by the group, not to hinder it. Effectively leading the meetings means knowing the right- and wrong- ways to use parliamentary motions. This can help to establish appropriate leadership style with the backing of established policies. This keeps discussion orderly and reduces members interrupting each other and talking over one another. Discussion can continue if needed. The leader should do it orderly and to the issue at hand.

Some of the more frequently used and obvious parliamentary errors are included below. Their use indicates that some members have a tenuous grasp on *Robert's Rules of Order* as they relate to dealing with motions. An effective leader should be able to provide guidance and teaching in these areas without embarrassing the speaker.

This list is outlined below:

- *Speaking without recognition:* Requiring that a member gets recognition from the chair is a means of keeping order and ensuring fairness.
The appropriate way to get recognition is to rise and address the chair ("Madam President" or "Mr. Chairman") and wait for proper acknowledgement.
- *Moving to "Table":* Many people think tabling a motion is tantamount to killing it. But the motion to Lay on the Table is used to set a motion aside temporarily in order to consider something else that is more pressing or urgent. If the desire is for the main motion to be killed, the motion should be to Postpone indefinitely.
- *Calling the question:* Often when the same arguments continue to go back and forth on a pending motion, inevitably someone will call out "Question! or "I call the question!" The presiding officer may take this opportunity to inform the members that calling the question requires a motion from a member after being recognized by the chair. It is appropriate for the presiding officer to wait until it is clear that no one else wishes to speak on the issue. It should be made clear that calling out "Question" without obtaining the floor is rude.
- *Tabling it until next month/next meeting:* Using the word "table" in this instance is an error. The member who makes this proposal usually wants to Postpone to a Certain Time, not Lay on the Table.

- *"Reconsidering" a vote:* When using Robert's Rules, reconsider has a specific meaning that is sometimes at odds with the word's meaning in dictionary usage.

  In a meeting run by Robert's Rules, you can reconsider only with respect to a decision made in the current meeting (or on the next day if the meeting/session runs for more than one day).
- *Requesting a point of information:* This parliamentary procedure is often interpreted to mean the member can get the floor to give information. A point of information is made to request information, not to provide the speaker with the opportunity to talk again.
- *Making a motion to accept or receive reports:* Except in some specific situations, it is not necessary to entertain motions to accept or receive reports after they are presented. Instead the presiding officer should simply thank the member making the report and move to the next item of business. A report may contain recommendations or suggestions that the group needs to take some specific action. In those cases, the presiding officer will state the question on the motion that arises from the report.
- *Moving to Dispense with the minutes:* The maker of the motion does not really want to dispense with the minutes. The real intent is to dispense with the reading of the minutes during the meeting. Minutes must be approved in order to become the official record of the organization.

Therefore, the reading of the minutes can be dispensed, but they should be passed out to members, corrections should be asked for and approved at some point in order to have a complete and official record of the meetings.

It helps if members have the minutes prior to the meeting so they have time to read them before the meeting.

- *Using "I so move" to put a motion on the floor.* When a motion is made it should propose the intended action as accurately and specifically as possible. For example, if the maker of the motion says, "I so move" in response to the presiding officer saying, "the chair will entertain a motion to have a 5k Run as our fundraiser." No motion has really been made. The actions of the motion should be clearly stated so that members will be sure about their vote. The maker of the motion should use a language like: I move that our club sponsor a 5k run for our fundraiser this year." This allows everyone to know exactly what is being voted for currently.

These parliamentary items used correctly will help the meeting run more smoothly. They also save a lot of time.

CHAPTER 11

ORGANIZATIONAL COMMUNICATIONS

Communication is a critical facet of any organization. Even one-on-one type of communication can create problems if there is not complete understanding between both parties. Effective leaders must be able to conceive and understand the goals set for the organization. But they must also be able to articulate them to the membership and others as needed.

Oral communication is important. Many are gifted with the ability to present themselves well as speakers or facilitators. Others need to join an organization such as *Toastmasters* to gain a greater grasp on the art of speakers. Then practice getting even better.

The effective leader will seek to establish an open communication environment within the organization.

An open communication environment is one in which all members of the organization feel free to share opinions, provide feedback, ask questions, and even critique at any level. *This communication hierarchy requires that the leader builds a trust level that is the foundation for all communication.* "When the trust level is high, communication is easy, instant, and effortless" says Stephen Covey, author of *The Seven Habits of Highly Effective People: Powerful Lessons in Powerful Change.*

The organizational leader that will be successful will have a vocabulary of words and phrases that can be used in a variety of settings to sell an idea, the organization, or yourself. Almost every conversation, speech given, or letter sent for your organization can be sales, recruiting, or support gaining message. Whether speaking or writing every opportunity should be made to ensure that there is a second level message that asks or tells the recipient to think well of you and your organization.

Courtesy, clarity, correctness, and persuasion are important, but the use of descriptive words, strong verbs, and appealing phrases often create the desirability of the recipient to give a positive response.

With a versatile organization, the leader can effectively reach different target audiences by speeches and letters with words and phrases tailored to their needs and your purposes. We want to provide with a reference point in examples mentioned in the next few pages.

It is our sincere hope that you have grasped a greater level of understanding about what it means to be an effective leader in an organization of color. Your level of insight, and influence will shift a generation.

We're counting on you!

WINNING WORDS USED BY LEADERS

Affiliation	*Facts*
Adaptable	*Features*
Advantages	*Flair*
Affordable	*Flexibility*
Analytical	*Genuine*
Attainable	*High quality*
Authentic	*Influential*
Benchmarking	*Informative*
Benefits	*Innovative*
Breakthrough	*Integrity*
Business	*Intuitive*
Intelligence	*Invaluable*
Choice	*Mitigating risk*
Classic	*Natural*
Collaborative	*Nomenclature*
Compassionate	*Objectives-based strategy*
Confident	*Offer*
Contemporary	*Opportunity*
Critical Thinking	*Open Minded*
Dazzling	*Optional*
Delightful	*Passionate*
Dependable	*People development*
Effective	*Personalization*
Entrepreneurial	*Pledge*
Exceptional	*Powerful*
Exciting	*Practical*
Exclusive	*Precision*
Exemplary	*Premium*
Expert	*Positive attitude*
Exquisite	*Problem solving*

WINNING WORDS USED BY LEADERS
(CONTINUED)

Productive
Professional
Proven
Quality
Resourceful
Reliable
Relevant
Results oriented
Rewarding
Satisfying
Sisterly
Sophisticated

State-of-the –arts
facilities
Stunning
Substantial
Successful
Tremendous
Time
Management
Transformation
Up to date
Useful
Valuable
Versatile

WINNING PHRASES USED BY LEADERS

Affiliated with

Add a new dimension to your life

All-out effort

An impressive collection of women

As a bonus to our sisterhood

Be the first to

Common goal

Cooperative spirit

Cutting edge

Direct your attention to

Discover for yourself

Enjoy the elegant styling of the ladies

Engineered for service

Make a dramatic difference in your life

Make it easy for yourself as you check us out

Makes any day special

Many advantages of

Money's worth

More than 90 years of service

Moving through these times of uncertainty

Now for the first time

Of importance to you

One reason among many to join

One of the largest and most respected

Outstanding features

WINNING PHRASES USED BY LEADERS
(CONTINUED)

Express your personality as a member of

Pride of accomplishment

Meticulously crafted and designed

Privileges include

For personal and business advancement

Professional quality always

Gain the satisfaction of knowing

Reward yourself with

Get full details from

See for yourself

Gives you your choice of organizational

Service to the community

Have the satisfaction of knowing you are among the best

Simple steps

If you accept this invitation

Take advantage of this opportunity

Indulge yourself by joining the best

Take a moment to look at this

Influence others by this choice

Take the gamble out of choosing

Pleased to be able to invite you

WINNING PHRASES USED BY LEADERS
(CONTINUED)

In these fast-moving times

Invite you to share in

I take pride in nominating

Join forces

Join the thousands of others who

Just a reminder that

Looking forward to seeing you

Time-tested

Timeless elegance
Top of the line
Treat yourself to

Under our simple plan

Unequalled organization and service
Unique opportunity

Urge you to

What better way to
With our compliments
Worthwhile cause

Contact Authors

Would you like to schedule a book signing or speaking event with the authors?

Complete one of the contact forms at www.drcassandraowens.com or www.helenjowens.com

Desire to Write a Book?

Contact our publisher at www.drnesintl.com

Made in the USA
Monee, IL
24 October 2021